A Beginners Guide
to
LaTeX

Learn LaTeX in Easy Tutorials

By

Chetan P. Shirore

Department of Mathematics,
K.T.H.M. College, Nashik

Contents

1 What is LaTeX?

LaTeX is a document *preparing* system for *high-quality* typesetting. It is used for Articles, Research Papers, Scientific and Technical Documents, Presentations, Law-Texts, Scorecards, Bills, Letters, Books, Reports and almost any form of publishing. LaTeX is undoubtedly the best document preparation system.The accuracy and precision of document content and layout is achieved in LaTeX. A high quality auto formatting of the content is perhaps the best feature in LaTeX. We just have to take care of the proper content and rest will be done by LaTeX.

2 Why LaTeX?

→ Open Source and Freeware

→ Available for Windows, Linux, Macintosh, Browsers, etc.

→ Low Sized documents with High Quality Outputs

→ Post Script and Pdf Outputs

→ Extremely Stable: Handles very large and complex documents Smoothly

→ Cross Referencing Capabilities : Figures, Tables, Equations, Index etc.

→ Automatic Numbering: Chapters, Sections, Figures, Equations etc.

→ Automatic Generations : List of Contents, List of Figures, Index, Bibliography etc.

→ A large number of Packages for Different types of Documents

→ Customisable with Macros and Packages

→ Same Output Anytime, Anywhere on Any Operating System

3 How to use this Book?

This book is intended for beginners of LaTeX. It is specially written keeping in mind the difficulties of those who are used to use Microsoft Word. Almost all tasks that one is used to do in MS word are covered. A simple principle is used: *Do it (Type it) ... Get it.*

Type tutorials (or copy and paste from pdf file to LaTeX editor) ... Compile and Check the Output ... Understand the things ... and you will learn LaTeX!

Caution!: This book is *NOT* for intermediate or advanced users of LaTeX!.

4 Creating Documents in LaTeX

For creating and viewing documents using LaTeX, two things are needed:
i) TeX Distribution ii) LaTeX Editor.

TeX viewers and LaTeX Editors are available across platforms: Windows, Linux, Mac OS, Browser-based and Android. For Windows Operating System, following is the list of some of popular TeX distributions and LaTeX editors. Many of LaTeX editors are freewares while some of them are sharewares.

TeX Distributions	LaTeX Editors
TeX Live	Texworks Editor, Texnic Centre, Tex Studio
MikTex	Winedt, Lyx, Texmaker, Winshell

To begin creating your documents you may use "Miktex + Texworks Editor" or "Miktex + Texnic Centre" or maybe "Miktex + Tex Studio".

5   Understanding Basics

There are very few basic things that you need to understand ... not more than two ...

A) **Command Format in LaTeX**

```
\CommandName[Optional Argmument]{Compulsory Argument}
                    OR
 \CommandName{Compulsory Argument}[Optional argument]
```

Every Command in LaTeX is of this form. It starts with Backslash followed by Command Name, Optional Arguments in Square Brackets (if any) and Compulsory Arguments in Curly Brackets(if any).

```
Examples:
\documentclass[11pt]{article}
\documentclass{article}
\documentclass{article}[11pt]
```

Tip: Latex commands are case sensitive and generally there is no space in commands.

B) **Environments in LaTeX**

```
\begin{environment}
...
...
\end{environment}
```

In LaTeX we always work in environments like this.

```
Examples:
\begin{document} ... \end{document}
\begin{equation} ... \end{equation}
\begin{tabular} ... \end{tabular}
```

Believe it or not ... if you clearly understood the above basics, half of the job is done. You are advised to read the above basics once again.

Remember:

A) \CommandName[Optional Argmument]{Compulsory Argument}

B) \begin{environment} ... \end{environment}

6 First Document

Type as in the following box.

```
\documentclass[11pt]{article}
\begin{document}
This is Our First Document.
\end{document}
```

Compile and Check the Output.

> This is Our First Document.

Congrats ...! First Document is Compiled and Produced Successfully.

7 Document Structure

```
\documentclass[ ]{ }
\usepackage[ ]{ }
\begin{document}
. . . . . . . . . . . . . . .
. . . . . . . . . . . . . .
\end{document}
```

Points to Note:

1. The area between \documentclass[ ]{} and \begin{document} is called the preamble. It includes used packages and commands that affect whole document.

2. The actual content is contained in \begin{document} ... \end{document}

8 Document Classes and Document Sectioning

There are several document classes available in LaTeX. Few of them are listed below.

article	for short reports, articles, research papers
report	for lengthy reports, thesis, small books
book	for books
letter	for writing letters
beamer	for presentations

The document sectioning can be done up to 7 levels.

Content Part	Level
Part	-1
Chapter	0
Section	1
Subsection	2
Subsection	3
Paragraph	4
Subparagraph	5

\part and \chapter are available only for report and book document classes.

The one document class that is constantly used in this book is article document class. A typical article document is one like the following.

```
\documentclass{article}
\begin{document}
\tableofcontents
\section{First section}
\section{Second section}
\subsection{A sub-section in II section}
\subsubsection[Deeper level]{A
sub-section at deeper level}
\section{Third Section}
\subsection{A subsection in III section}
\subsection{Another subsection in III
    section}
\end{document}
```

Contents

1 First section

2 Second section

2.1 A sub-section in II section

2.1.1 A sub-section at deeper level

3 Third Section

3.1 A subsection in III section

3.2 Another subsection in III section

9 Line Break or New Line

```
\documentclass{article}
\begin{document}
First Sentence in a Line.
Second Sentence in Same Line.\\
First Sentence in a Line. \\
Second Sentence in New Line.
\end{document}
```

First Sentence in a Line. Second Sentence in Same Line.

First Sentence in a Line.
Second Sentence New Line.

Key Point: A doubleslash \\ is used for New Line. The alternative is to use \newline. Similarly, \newpage is used for New Page.

10 New Paragraph

```
\documentclass{article}
\begin{document}
I Sentence in I Paragraph.\\
II Sentence in New Line but in Same
    Paragraph.
\end{document}
```

I Sentence in I Paragraph.
II Sentence in New Line but in Same Paragraph.

```
\documentclass{article}
\begin{document}
I Sentence in I Paragraph.

II Sentence in New Paragraph.
\end{document}
```

I Sentence in I Paragraph.

II Sentence in New Paragraph.

Key Point: A *blank line* is used for new paragraph.

Points to Understand

A) Multiple Spaces are equivalent to Single Space in LaTeX. For example,
   How Are You?
   and
   How   Are   You ?
   produce same viz. How Are You?

B) Multiple Blank Lines are equivalent to Single Blank Line in LaTeX. For Example,
   This is First Sentence.

   This is Second Sentence.
   and
   This is First Sentence.

This is Second Sentence.

produce same viz.
This is First Sentence.
This is Second Sentence.

Tips:

1. For manually adding spaces, type backslash and space (\ ). It acts as Spacebar in LaTeX.

2. For manually adding blank lines, type backslash two times (\\). It acts as Enter in LaTeX.

11 Font Styles

```
\documentclass{article}
\begin{document}

\textbf{This is text in Bold font.}      This is text in Bold font.

\textit{This is text in Italic font.}     This is text in Italic font.

\underline{This is Underlined text.}      This is Underlined text.

\emph{This is Emphasized text.}           This is Emphasized text.

\textsl{This is Slanted text.}            This is Slanted text.

\end{document}
```

12   Special Symbols

```
\documentclass{article}

\begin{document}

\# \$ \% \{ \} \& \_ \textbackslash \textendash \textemdash    # $ % { } & _ \ – —

\copyright \textregistered \texttrademark                      © ® ™

\end{document}
```

Key Point: For typing out many of special symbols, we just have to type \ before it.

13   Different Fonts

```
\documentclass{article}

\begin{document}

\texttt {A text in Typewriter Font.}    A text in Typewriter Font.

\textsf{A text in Serif Font.}          A text in Serif Font.

\textrm{A text in Roman Font.}          A text in Roman Font.

\end{document}
```

14　Font Size

```
\documentclass{article}

\begin{document}

\tiny Tiny, \scriptsize Scriptsize          Tiny, Scriptsize

\footnotesize Footnotesize, \small Small    Footnotesize, Small

\normalsize Normal                          Normal

\large Large, \Large Larger                 Large, Larger

 \huge Largest, \Huge Largest              Largest, Largest

\end{document}
```

15　Subscript and Superscript

```
\documentclass{article}
\usepackage{fixltx2e}
\begin{document}

A \textsuperscript{superscript} text.     A superscript text.

A \textsubscript{subscript} text.         A subscript text.

\end{document}
```

Key Point A superscript text is done with \textsuperscript. A subscript text is done with \textsubscript in package *fixltx2e*.

16   Alignments

```
\documentclass{article}

\begin{document}
\begin{flushleft}
This is Flushed Left text.
\end{flushleft}
```

This is Flushed Left text.

```
This is Normally Aligned text.
```

This is Normally Aligned text.

```
\begin{center}
This is Center Aligned Text.
\end{center}
```

This is Center Aligned Text.

```
\begin{flushright}
This is Flushed Right text.
\end{flushright}
```

This is Flushed Right text.

```
\end{document}
```

17   Adding Horizontal and Vertical Space

```
\documentclass{article}
\begin{document}
A horizontal \hspace{10pt} space of 10 points.\\
A horizontal \hspace{2cm} space of 2 cm.\\

A first Paragraph.

 \vspace{1cm}
A second Pargraph with additional space of 1cm.
\end{document}
```

A horizontal   space of 10 points.
A horizontal   space of 2 cm.

A first Paragraph.

A second Pargraph with additional space of 1cm.

Key Point: \hspace for horizontal space and \vspace for vertical space.

18   Including Comments in Documents

Comments may be added in TeX documents at appropriate places. They are useful while reviewing or editing source codes.

```
\documentclass{article}
\begin{document}
The  part % comment
% a comment line
is not printed as it is a comment.
\end{document}
```

The next part is not printed as it is a comment.

```
\documentclass{article}
\usepackage{comment}
\begin{document}
The next part is of comments
\begin{comment}
A first line of comment.
A second line of comment.
\end{comment}
which does not get printed in output.
\end{document}
```

The next part is of comments which does not get printed in output.

Points to Understand:

1. % to include comments. The next part after percentage sign in a line is comment.

2. package *comment* for including multi line comments.

---

19   Page Layout

```
\documentclass{article}
\begin{document}
This is a sample document.
\end{document}
```

With above, a document is produced having default parameters as
Paper Size: Letter, Font: Computer Modern, Font Size: 10pt., Orientation: Portrait, One Column

```
\documentclass[12pt]{article}
\usepackage[a4paper,landscape]{geometry}
\begin{document}
This is a sample document.
\end{document}
```

With above, a document is produced having parameters as
Paper Size: A4, Font: Computer Modern, Font Size: 12pt., Orientation: Landscape, One Column

```
\documentclass[14pt,twocolumn]{article}
\usepackage[legalpaper,landscape]{geometry}
\begin{document}
This is a sample document.
\end{document}
```

With above, a document is produced having parameters as
Paper Size: Legal, Font: Computer Modern, Font Size: 14pt., Orientation: Landscape, Two
Columns

```
\documentclass[14pt,twocolumn]{article}
\usepackage[paperheight=11in,paperwidth=8.5in,landscape,
    left=1in,right=1in,top=1in,bottom=1cm]{geometry}
\begin{document}
This is a sample document.
\end{document}
```

With above, a document is produced having parameters as
Paper Height: 11 inch, Paper Width: 8.5 inch, Font: Computer Modern, Font Size: 14pt.,
Orientation: Landscape, Two Columns, Left Margin: 1 inch, Right Margin: 1 inch, Top
Margin: 1 inch, Bottom Margin : 1 cm

Different Page Size in LaTeX : a0paper, a1paper, ..., a6paper; b0paper, b1paper, ...,
b6paper, letterpaper, legalpaper, ...

Different Document Classes in LaTeX: Article, Letter, Book, Report, Slides , Beamer
etc.

Key Point: Use *Geometry Package* for Selecting Paper Size, Setting Margins, Orientation.

20 Drawing Horizontal Line

```
\documentclass{article}
\begin{document}

\rule{\linewidth}{1pt}

\end{document}
```

Points to Understand: The command format is

```
\rule[raise-height]{width}{thickness}
```

1. raise height specifies how high to raise the rule (optional).

2. width specifies the length of the rule (mandatory).

3. thickness specifies the thickness of the rule (mandatory).

21 Colouring Text

```
\documentclass{article}
\usepackage{color}
\begin{document}

 \color{red}{Red} \dots \color{blue} {Blue}          Red ... Blue ...
     \dots \color{green} {Green}

\end{document}
```

Key Point: Use package *color* for colouring text.

Point to Understand: The command format is

```
\color{declared-color}{text}
```

Tip: Set page background color with \pagecolor{color}using *color* package.

22 Bullets and Numbering

```
\documentclass{article}        \documentclass{article}        \documentclass{article}
\begin{document}               \begin{document}               \usepackage{enumitem}
                                                              \begin{document}


\textbf{Simple List}           \textbf{Numbered List}         \textbf{List with Small Alphabets}
\begin{itemize}                \begin{enumerate}              \begin{enumerate}[label=\alph*.]
\item First Member             \item First Member             \item First Member
\item Second Member            \item Second Member            \item Second Member
\item Third Member             \item Third Member             \item Third Member
\end{itemize}                  \end{enumerate}                \end{enumerate}


\end{document}                 \end{document}                 \end{document}
```

Simple List
- First Member
- Second Member
- Third Member

Numbered List
1. First Member
2. Second Member
3. Third Member

List with Small Alphabets
a. First Member
b. Second Member
c. Third Member

```
\documentclass{article}                    \documentclass{article}
\usepackage{enumitem}                      \usepackage{enumitem}
\begin{document}                           \begin{document}

\textbf{List with Small Roman Numbers}     \textbf{List with Capital Alphabets}
\begin{enumerate}[label=\roman*.]          \begin{enumerate}[label=\Alph*)]
\item First Member                         \item First Member
\item Second Member                        \item Second Member
\item Third Member                         \item Third Member
\end{enumerate}                            \end{enumerate}

\end{document}                             \end{document}
```

List with Small Roman Numbers

    i. First Member

   ii. Second Member

  iii. Third Member

List with Capital Alphabets

  A) First Member

  B) Second Member

  C) Third Member

Tip: [label = {}] for unlabelled lists.

```
\documentclass{article}
\usepackage{enumitem}
\begin{document}
\textbf{List with Capital Roman
    Numbers Starting at 3}
\begin{enumerate}[label=\Roman*.,start=3]
\item First Member
\item Second Member
\item Third Member
\end{enumerate}
\end{document}
```

```
\documentclass{article}
\usepackage{paralist}
\begin{document}
\textbf{Numbered List IN A PARAGRAPH :}
A list in paragraph.
\begin{inparaenum}
\item First Member
\item Second Member
\item Third Member.
\end{inparaenum}
\end{document}
```

List with Capital Roman Numbers Starting at 3
  III. First Member
  IV. Second Member
   V. Third Member

Numbered List IN A PARAGRAPH : A list in paragraph. 1. First 2. Second 3. Third

```
\documentclass{article}
\usepackage{paralist}
\begin{document}
\textbf{List IN A PARAGRAPH with Small
    Alphabets}
This is a list in a paragraph.
\begin{inparaenum}[a)]
\item First Member
\item Second Member
\item Third Member.
\end{inparaenum}
\end{document}
```

```
\documentclass{article}
\begin{document}
\textbf{Nested List}
\begin{itemize}
\item First Memeber of Main List
\item Second Member of Main List
\item Third Member of Main List
\begin{itemize}
\item First Member of Sublist of III Member
\item Second Member of Sublist of III Member
\end{itemize}
\item Fourth and Last Member of Main List
\end{itemize}
\end{document}
```

List IN A PARAGRAPH with Small Alphabets This is a list in a paragraph. a) First Member b) Second Member c) Third Member.

Nested List
- First Memeber of Main List
- Second Member of Main List
- Third Member of Main List
  - First Member of Sublist of III Member
  - Second Member of Sublist of III Member
- Fourth and Last Member of Main List

Key Points:

1. Use package *enumitem* for bullets and numbering.

2. Use package *paralist* for bullets and numbering inside a paragraph.

23   Listing Theorems, Definitions, Examples etc.

```
\documentclass{article}
\usepackage{paralist}
\begin{document}

\textbf{Def\/inition List Inside
    Paragraph:}
\begin{inparadesc}
\item[First Def\/inition:]A first
    def\/inition.
\item[Second Def\/inition:]A second
    def\/inition.
\item[Third Def\/inition:]A third
    def\/inition.
\end{inparadesc}

\end{document}
```

```
\documentclass{article}
\begin{document}

\textbf{Simple Def\/inition List.}
\begin{description}
\item[First Def\/inition:]A first def\/inition.
\item[Second Def\/inition:]A second def\/inition.
\item[Third Def\/inition:]A third def\/inition.
\end{description}

\end{document}
```

Inside Paragraph: First Definition: A first definition. **Second Definition:** A second definition. **Third Definition:** A third definition.

Simple Definition List.
First Definition: A first definition.
Second Definition: A second definition.
Third Definition: A third definition.

Key Points:

1. For Theorems,Definitions, Examples etc. use

   \begin{description}...\end{description}

2. Use package *inparadesc* For Theorems,Definitions, Examples etc. inside a paragraph.

Point to Understand: f \ / i is used for proper spacing between letters f and i.

```
\documentclass{article}
\usepackage{amsmath}
\begin{document}
\newtheorem{thmv}{Theorem}
\newtheorem{dfnb}{Definition}
\newtheorem{lem}{Lemma}
\begin{thmv}
This is a theorem.
\end{thmv}
\begin{thmv}
This is another theorem.
\end{thmv}
\begin{dfnb}
This is definition.
\end{dfnb}
\begin{dfnb}
This is another definition.
\end{dfnb}
\begin{lem}
This is lemma.
\end{lem}
\end{document}
```

Theorem 1 *This is a theorem.*
Theorem 2 *This is another theorem.*
Definition 1 *This is definition.*
Definition 2 *This is another definition.*
Lemma 1 *This is lemma.*

Points to Understand: The command format is

```
\newtheorem{nickname of environment}{name of environment as to be
    printed}[within]
                            OR
\newtheorem{nickname of environment}[numbered like]{name of environment as to
    be printed}
```

1. within: The name of an already defined counter, usually of a sectional unit. For example,

   ```
   \newtheorem{thmv}{Theorem}[section]
   ```

   prefixes a section number before theorem number.

2. numbered like: The name of an already defined theorem-like environment.For example,

   ```
   \newtheorem{thmv}{Theorem}[section]
   \newtheorem{dfnb}[thmv]{Definition}
   ```

   Here a counter of theorem environment(along with its formatting) is used to number definitions. It is useful when separate numbering is not required for theorems, definitions, examples etc. specially within a section.

25   Tabs in LaTeX

```
\documentclass{article}
\begin{document}
\begin{tabbing}
\= Tab1 \= Tab2 \= Tab3 \= Tab4 \= Tab5 \= Tab6 \\
\> Tab1 \\
\> \>Tab2 \\
\> \> \> Tab3 \\
 \> \> \> \> Tab4 \\
 \> \> \> \> \> Tab5 \\
 \> \> \> \> \> \> Tab6
\end{tabbing}
\end{document}
```

Tab1 Tab2 Tab3 Tab4 Tab5 Tab6
Tab1
    Tab2
        Tab3
            Tab4
                Tab5
                    Tab6

Key Points:

1. Use \= to *SET* tab positions.

2. Use \> to *MOVE* to tab positions.

---

26   URLs,Hyperlinks and Bookmarks

```
\documentclass[a4paper,12pt]{article}
\usepackage{url}p
\begin{document}
\section{First Section}
\section{Second Section}
\url{www.somewebsiteaddress.com}
\subsection{A subsection}
\end{document}
```

1   First Section

2   Second Section

www.somewebsiteaddress.com

2.1   A subsection

Key Point: *url* package for urls. The command format is

```
\url{link-address}
```

It prints out url with link.

```
\documentclass[a4paper,12pt]{article}
\usepackage{url,hyperref}
\begin{document}
\section{First Section}
\href{www.somewebsiteaddress.com}{some
text pointing to url}\\
\section{Second Section}
\url{www.somewebsiteaddress.com}\\
\subsection{A subsection}
\nolinkurl{www.somewebsiteaddress.com}
\end{document}
```

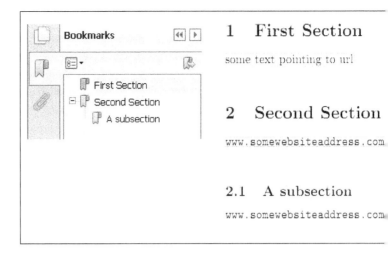

```
\documentclass[a4paper,12pt]{article}
\usepackage{url,hyperref}
\documentclass[a4paper,12pt]{article}
\usepackage{url}
\usepackage[colorlinks=true]{hyperref}
\begin{document}
\section{First Section}
\href{www.somewebsiteaddress.com}{some
text pointing to url}\\
\section{Second Section}
\url{www.somewebsiteaddress.com}\\
\subsection{A subsection}
\nolinkurl{www.somewebsiteaddress.com}
\end{document}
```

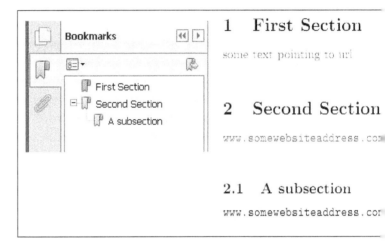

Key Point: *hyperref* package creates auto bookmarks and hyperlinks. It has optional arguments to change appearance of bookmarks and hyperlinks.

27 Header and Footer

27.1 Header and Footer for all pages

```
\documentclass{article}
\usepackage{fancyhdr}
\pagestyle{fancy}
\renewcommand{\headrulewidth}{0pt}
\lhead{Left Header}
\chead{Center Header}
\rhead{Right Header}
\lfoot{Left Footer}
\cfoot{Center Footer}
\rfoot{Right Footer}
\begin{document}

This is content part.

\end{document}
```

Left Header	Center Header	Right Header
This is Content Part.		
Left Footer	Center Footer	Right Footer

```
\documentclass{article}
\usepackage{fancyhdr}
\pagestyle{fancy}
\renewcommand{\headrulewidth}{0pt}
\lhead{Left Header}
\chead{Center Header}
\rhead{Right Header}
\lfoot{Left Footer}
\cfoot{Page \thepage}
\rfoot{Right Footer}
\begin{document}

This is content part.

\end{document}
```

Left Header	Center Header	Right Header
This is Content Part.		
Left Footer	Page 1	Right Footer

Key Point: Use package *fancyhdr* for Header and Footer.

> **Point to Understand:** \renewcommand {\headrulewidth}{0pt} is used to remove line after header.

27.2 Customising Headers and Footers for different pages

```
\documentclass{article}
\usepackage{fancyhdr}
\pagestyle{fancy}
\renewcommand{\headrulewidth}{0pt}
\lhead{Left Header}
\chead{Center Header}
\rhead{Right Header}
\lfoot{Left Footer}
\cfoot{Page \thepage}
\rfoot{Right Footer}
\begin{document}
First page with header and footer.
\newpage
\thispagestyle{empty}
Second page without header and footer.
\end{document}
```

Left Header	Center Header	Right Header
First page with header and footer.		
Left Footer	Page 1	Right Footer

Second page without header and footer.

Point to Understand: \thispagestyle{empty}to remove header and footer from the current page.

```
\documentclass{article}
\usepackage{fancyhdr}
\pagestyle{fancy}
\renewcommand{\headrulewidth}{0pt}
\lhead{Left Header}
\chead{Center Header}
\rhead{Right Header}
\lfoot{Left Footer}
\cfoot{Page \thepage}
\rfoot{Right Footer}
\fancypagestyle{mystyle}
{\fancyhf{}
\fancyhead[l]{New Left Header}
\fancyhead[c]{New Center Header}
\fancyhead[r]{New Right Header}
\fancyfoot[l]{New Left Footer}
\fancyfoot[c]{New Center Footer}
\fancyfoot[r]{New Right Footer}}
\begin{document}
First page with header and footer.
\newpage
\thispagestyle{mystyle}
Second page with new header and
    footer.
\end{document}
```

Left Header	Center Header	Right Header
First page with header and footer.		
Left Footer	Page 1	Right Footer

New Left Header	New Center Header	New Right Header
Second page with new header and footer.		
New Left Footer	New Center Footer	New Right Footer

28 Tables

28.1 Simple Tables

```
\documentclass{article}
\begin{document}

\textbf{Table: 3 cols. (Center Aligned)}\\

\begin{tabular}{ccc}
\hline
\textbf{Col. 1}&\textbf{Col. 2}& \textbf{Col. 3}\\
\hline
11 & 12 & 13 \\
\hline
21 & 22 & 23 \\
\hline
31 & 32 & 33 \\
\hline
\end{tabular}\\

\end{document}
```

Table: 3 cols. (Center Aligned)

Col. 1	Col. 2	Col. 3
11	12	13
21	22	23
31	32	33

```
\documentclass{article}
\begin{document}
\textbf{Table: 3 cols. (Right Aligned)}\\

\begin{tabular}{rrr}
\hline
\textbf{Col. 1} & \textbf{Col. 2} & \textbf{Col. 3} \\
\hline
11 & 12 & 13 \\
\hline
21 & 22 & 23 \\
\hline
31 & 32 & 33 \\
\hline
\end{tabular}\\
\end{document}
```

Table: 3 cols. (Right Aligned)

Col. 1	Col. 2	Col. 3
11	12	13
21	22	23
31	32	33

```
\documentclass{article}
\begin{document}
\textbf{Table: 3 cols. (Left Aligned)}\\

\begin{tabular}{lll}
\hline
\textbf{Col. 1} & \textbf{Col. 2} & \textbf{Col. 3} \\
\hline
11 & 12 & 13 \\
\hline
21 & 22 & 23 \\
\hline
31 & 32 & 33 \\
\hline
\end{tabular}\\
\end{document}
```

Table: 3 cols. (Left Aligned)

Col. 1	Col. 2	Col. 3
11	12	13
21	22	23
31	32	33

```
\documentclass{article}
\begin{document}
\textbf{Table: 3 cols. (Fixed Width)}\\

\begin{tabular}{p{1.5cm}p{2cm}p{1.5cm}}
\hline
\textbf{Col. 1} & \textbf{Col. 2} & \textbf{Col. 3} \\
\hline
11 & 12 & 13 \\
\hline
21 & 22 & 23 \\
\hline
31 & 32 & 33 \\
\hline
\end{tabular}\\
\end{document}
```

Table: 3 cols. (Fixed Width)

Col. 1	Col. 2	Col. 3
11	12	13
21	22	23
31	32	33

```
\documentclass{article}
\begin{document}
\textbf{Table: 3 cols. (Center Aligned)}\\

\begin{tabular}{|c|c|c|}
\hline
\textbf{Col. 1} & \textbf{Col. 2} & \textbf{Col. 3} \\
\hline
11 & 12 & 13 \\
\hline
21 & 22 & 23 \\
\hline
31 & 32 & 33 \\
\hline
\end{tabular}\\
\end{document}
```

Table: 3 cols. (Center Aligned)

Col. 1	Col. 2	Col. 3
11	12	13
21	22	23
31	32	33

```
\documentclass{article}
\begin{document}
\textbf{Table: 3 columns (Right Aligned)}\\

\begin{tabular}{|r|r|r|}
\hline
\textbf{Col. 1} & \textbf{Col. 2} & \textbf{Col. 3} \\
\hline
11 & 12 & 13 \\
\hline
21 & 22 & 23 \\
\hline
31 & 32 & 33 \\
\hline
\end{tabular}\\
\end{document}
```

Table: 3 cols. (Right Aligned)

Col. 1	Col. 2	Col. 3
11	12	13
21	22	23
31	32	33

```
\documentclass{article}
\begin{document}
\textbf{Table: 3 cols. (Left Aligned)}\\

\begin{tabular}{|l|l|l|}
\hline
\textbf{Col. 1} & \textbf{Col. 2} & \textbf{Col. 3} \\
\hline
11 & 12 & 13 \\
\hline
21 & 22 & 23 \\
\hline
31 & 32 & 33 \\
\hline
\end{tabular}\\
\end{document}
```

Table: 3 cols. (Left Aligned)

Col. 1	Col. 2	Col. 3
11	12	13
21	22	23
31	32	33

```
\documentclass{article}
\begin{document}

\textbf{Table: 3 cols. (Fixed Width)}\\

\begin{tabular}{|p{1.5cm}|p{2cm}|p{1.5cm}|}
\hline
\textbf{Col. 1} & \textbf{Col. 2} & \textbf{Col. 3} \\
\hline
11 & 12 & 13 \\
\hline
21 & 22 & 23 \\
\hline
31 & 32 & 33 \\
\hline
\end{tabular}\\

\end{document}
```

Table: 3 cols. (Fixed Width)

Col. 1	Col. 2	Col. 3
11	12	13
21	22	23
31	32	33

Tip: Avoid vertical lines in tables for better readability of content.

28.2   Aligning Cells

```
\documentclass{article}
\usepackage{array}
\begin{document}

\textbf{Cell Alignment:}\\

\begin{tabular}{|b{1.6cm}|m{1.6cm}|p{1.6cm}|}
\hline
top aligned & middle aligned & bottom aligned\\
\hline
\end{tabular}

\end{document}
```

Cell Alignment:

top aligned	middle aligned	bottom aligned

Key Point: Alignment of cells is done with *array* package.

28.3 Row Height

```
\documentclass{article}
\usepackage{array}
\begin{document}
\setlength{\extrarowheight}{4pt}
\begin{tabular}{|c|c|c|}
\hline
11 & 12 & 13\\
\hline
21 & 22 & 23 \\
\hline
\end{tabular}
\end{document}
```

11	12	13
21	22	23

```
\documentclass{article}
\usepackage{array}
\begin{document}
\setlength{\extrarowheight}{16pt}
\begin{tabular}{|c|c|c|}
\hline
11 & 12 & 13\\
\hline
21 & 22 & 23 \\
\hline
\end{tabular}
\end{document}
```

11	12	13
21	22	23

Key Point: Use \setlength in *array* package to set row height.

28.4 Adding Blank Line in a Row

```
\documentclass{article}
\usepackage{array}
\begin{document}

\begin{tabular}{ccc}
\hline
\textbf{Col. 1} & \textbf{Col. 2} & \textbf{Col. 3} \\
\hline
11 & 12 & 13 \\
\hline
21 & 22 & 23 \\
&\\
\hline
31 & 32 & 33 \\
\hline
\end{tabular}
\end{document}
```

Col. 1	Col. 2	Col. 3
11	12	13
21	22	23
31	32	33

Key Point: Use &\\ to add blank line.

28.5 Slashbox in a table

```
\documentclass{article}
\usepackage{slashbox}
\begin{document}

\begin{tabular}{|c|c|c|}
\hline
\backslashbox{row}{column} & B & C \\
\hline
11 & 12 & 13 \\
\hline
21 & 22 & 23 \\
\hline
31 & 32 & 33 \\
\hline
\end{tabular}

\end{document}
```

row \ column	B	C
11	12	13
21	22	23
31	32	33

Key Point: Use *slashbox* package for slashbox in a table.

28.6   Beautiful Tables with *booktabs* package

```
\documentclass{article}
\usepackage{booktabs}
\begin{document}

\begin{tabular}{ccc}
\toprule[1.5pt]
A & B & C \\
\midrule
11 & 12 & 13 \\
21 & 22 & 23 \\
31 & 32 & 33 \\
\bottomrule[1.5pt]
\end{tabular}

\end{document}
```

A	B	C
11	12	13
21	22	23
31	32	33

Have beautiful tables with *booktabs* package!

28.7   Merging Cells in a Row

```
\documentclass{article}
\begin{document}

\begin{tabular}{ccc}
\hline
\multicolumn{2}{l}{Combined Column}&
\multicolumn{1}{l}{Last Column}\\
\hline
11 & 12 & 13 \\
21 & 22 & 23 \\
31 & 32 & 33 \\
\hline
\end{tabular}

\end{document}
```

Combined Column		Last Column
11	12	13
21	22	23
31	32	33

Key Point: Use \multicolumn for merging cells in a row. The command format is

$$\multicolumn\{cols\}\{pos\}\{text\}$$

1. cols specifies the number of columns to span.

2. pos specifies the formatting of the entry; c for centred, l for left, r for right.

3. text specifies what text is to make up the entry.

```
\documentclass{article}
\begin{document}

\begin{tabular}{ccc}
\hline
\multicolumn{2}{l}{Combined Column}&
\multicolumn{1}{l}{Last Column}\\
\cline{1-2}
11 & 12 & 13 \\
21 & 22 & 23 \\
31 & 32 & 33 \\
\hline
\end{tabular}

\end{document}
```

Combined Column		Last Column
11	12	13
21	22	23
31	32	33

Point to Understand: \cline is used to draw horizontal line from first column to second column after first row.

```
\documentclass{article}
\usepackage{booktabs}
\begin{document}

\begin{tabular}{ccc}
\toprule[1.5pt]
\multicolumn{2}{l}{Combined Column}&
\multicolumn{1}{l}{Last Column}\\
A & B & C\\
 \cmidrule(r){1-2}\cmidrule(l){3-3}
11 & 12 & 13 \\
21 & 22 & 23 \\
31 & 32 & 33 \\
\bottomrule[1.5pt]
\end{tabular}

\end{document}
```

Combined Column		Last Column
A	B	C
11	12	13
21	22	23
31	32	33

Booktabs package for beautiful tables!

28.8 Merging Cells in a Column

```
\documentclass{article}
\usepackage{multirow}
\begin{document}

\begin{tabular}{cccc}
\hline
\multirow{2}{*}{Combined Row} & A & 11 & 12\\
& B & 21 & 22 \\
\hline
\multirow{1}{*}{Last Row} & C & 31 & 32 \\
\hline
\end{tabular}

\end{document}
```

	A	11	12
Combined Row	B	21	22
Last Row	C	31	32

Key Point: Use package *multirow* for merging cells in a column.

$$\text{\multirow\{numrows\}\{width\}\{content\}}$$

1. `numrows` specifies the number of rows to span.

2. `width` specifies the width of the entry; * is used for natural width.

3. `content` specifies what text is to make up the entry.

```
\documentclass{article}
\usepackage{booktabs}
\usepackage{multirow}
\begin{document}

\begin{tabular}{cccc}
\toprule[1.5pt]
\multirow{2}{*}{Combined Row} & A & 11 & 12\\
& B & 21 & 22 \\
\hline
\multirow{1}{*}{Last Row} & C & 31 & 32 \\
\bottomrule[1.5pt]
\end{tabular}

\end{document}
```

	A	11	12
Combined Row	B	21	22
Last Row	C	31	32

28.9   Naming Tables

```
\documentclass{article}
\begin{document}

\begin{table}[htbp]
\begin{tabular}{ccc}
\hline
\textbf{Col. 1} & \textbf{Col. 2} & \textbf{Col. 3} \\
\hline
11 & 12 & 13 \\
\hline
21 & 22 & 23 \\
\hline
31 & 32 & 33 \\
\hline
\end{tabular}
\centering
\caption{Table Name - Below}
\end{table}

\end{document}
```

Col. 1	Col. 2	Col. 3
11	12	13
21	22	23
31	32	33

Table 1: Table Name - Below

```
\documentclass{article}
\begin{document}
\begin{table}[htbp]
\centering
\caption{Table Name - Above}
\vspace{10pt}
\begin{tabular}{ccc}
\hline
\textbf{Col. 1} & \textbf{Col. 2} & \textbf{Col. 3} \\
\hline
11 & 12 & 13 \\
\hline
21 & 22 & 23 \\
\hline
31 & 32 & 33 \\
\hline
\end{tabular}\\
\end{table}
\end{document}
```

Table 1: Table Name - Above

Col. 1	Col. 2	Col. 3
11	12	13
21	22	23
31	32	33

Point to Understand: Put *tabular* environment in *table* environment. Use \caption before or after *tabular* environment.

28.10   Colouring Tables

```
\documentclass{article}          \documentclass{article}          \documentclass{article}
\usepackage{colortbl}            \usepackage{colortbl}            \usepackage{colortbl}
\begin{document}                 \begin{document}                 \begin{document}
\begin{tabular}{ccc}             \begin{tabular}                  \begin{tabular}
\hline                           {>{\columncolor{red}}c>             {>{\columncolor{red}}c>
\rowcolor{red}                   {\columncolor{blue}}c>            {\columncolor{blue}}c>
11 & 12 & 13 \\                  {\columncolor{green}}c}          {\color{yellow}\columncolor{green}}c}
\hline                           \hline                           \hline
\rowcolor{blue}                  11 & 12 & 13 \\                  11 & 12 & 13 \\
21 & 22 & 23 \\                  \hline                           \hline
\hline                           21 & 22 & 23 \\                  21 & 22 & 23 \\
\rowcolor{green}                 \hline                           \hline
31 & 32 & 33 \\                  31 & 32 & 33 \\                  31 & 32 & 33 \\
\hline                           \hline                           \hline
\end{tabular}                    \end{tabular}                    \end{tabular}
\end{document}                   \end{document}                   \end{document}
```

11	12	13
21	22	23
31	32	33

11	12	13
21	22	23
31	32	33

11	12	
21	22	
31	32	

Key Point: Use *colortbl* package for colouring table contents.

29   Including Figures

```
\documentclass{article}
\usepackage{graphicx}
\begin{document}

\begin{figure}[htbp]
\begin{center}
\includegraphics[width=0.3\textwidth,
    angle=0]{sample.jpg}
\caption{Sample Figure}
\end{center}
\end{figure}

\end{document}
```

Figure 1: Sample Figure

```
\documentclass{article}
\usepackage{graphicx}
\begin{document}

\begin{figure}[htbp]
\begin{center}
\fbox{\includegraphics[width=3cm, angle=0]{sample.jpg}}
\caption{Sample Figure}
\end{center}
\end{figure}

\end{document}
```

Figure 2: Sample Figure

Key Point: Use *graphicx* package for including figures.

Points to Understand:

1. Here the sample image is placed in the folder where the tex file is.

2. 0.3\width denotes 30% of total page width.

3. \fbox is used to frame the figure. It can also be used to frame the text.

30 Mathematics Environment in LaTeX

30.1 Understanding Basics

a) \(... \)   OR $ ... $

   creates *INLINE* mathematics environment.

b) \[... \]   OR $$ ... $$

   creates mathematics environment in *NEW LINE.*

c) \begin{equation} ... \end{equation}

   creates mathematics environment in *NEW LINE* with *numbered equations.*

You are strongly advised to read the above basics at least once.

Tip: Try to avoid use of $ ... $ OR $$ ... $$.

```
\documentclass{article}
\begin{document}
Equations are \( a + b = c \)
and \( x + y = z \)
\end{document}
```

Equations are $a + b = c$ and $x + y = z$

```
\documentclass{article}
\begin{document}
Equations are \[ a + b = c \]
and \[ x + y = z \]
\end{document}
```

Equations are

$$a + b = c$$

and

$$x + y = z$$

```
\documentclass{article}
\begin{document}
Equations are
\begin{equation}
 a + b = c
\end{equation}
\begin{equation}
 a + b = c
\end{equation}
\end{document}
```

Equations are

$$a + b = c \qquad (1)$$

$$x + y = z \qquad (2)$$

30.2 Aligning Equations

```
\documentclass{article}
\usepackage{amsmath}
\begin{document}
\begin{multline}
x = a + b + c + d + e+ \\
f + g + h + i + j+ \\
k + l + m + n
\end{multline}

\begin{gather}
x + y + z = 0\\
y + z = 1
\end{gather}

\begin{align}
x + y + z = 1\\
y + z = 0\\
u + v + w + z =2
\end{align}

\begin{equation}
\begin{split}
a = b\\
=c\\
\end{split}
\end{equation}
\end{document}
```

$$x = a+b+c+d+e+$$
$$f+g+h+i+j+$$
$$k+l+m+n \quad (3)$$

$$x+y+z = 0 \quad (4)$$
$$y+z = 1 \quad (5)$$

$$x+y+z = 1 \quad (6)$$
$$y+z = 0 \quad (7)$$
$$u+v+w+z = 2 \quad (8)$$

$$a = b$$
$$= c \quad (9)$$

Points to Understand:

1. Alignment of Equations is done with *amsmath* package.

2. *Multiline* is used for equations longer than a line.

3. *Gather* is used to centre align list of equations.

4. *Align* is used to vertically align the equations w.r.t. $<$, $>$, $=$ etc.

5. *Split* is used to align right hand sides of equations w.r.t. $<$, $>$, $=$ etc.

Tips:

a) Use asterisk for *unnumbered* equations;

   \begin{equation*},\begin{multiline*}, \begin{gather*}, \begin{align*}

b) Use \nonumber for some *unnumbered* equation\expression in set of numbered equations\expressions.

30.3   Greek Letters

```
\documentclass{article}
\begin{document}
\[\alpha, \beta, \gamma, \delta, \rho, \lambda, \Delta, \nabla\]     $\alpha, \beta, \gamma, \delta, \rho, \lambda, \Delta, \nabla$
\[\epsilon, \theta, \eta, \tau, \pi, \sigma, \phi, \xi\]     $\epsilon, \theta, \eta, \tau, \pi, \sigma, \phi, \xi$
\end{document}
```

30.4   Common Sets

```
\documentclass{article}
\usepackage{bbm}
\begin{document}
\[\mathbbm{C,Z,Q,R, N, Z_+, R^+} \]     $\mathbb{C}, \mathbb{Z}, \mathbb{Q}, \mathbb{R}, \mathbb{N}, \mathbb{Z}_+, \mathbb{R}^+$
\[\mathcal{A}, \mathcal{S}, \mathcal{T} \]     $\mathcal{A}, \mathcal{S}, \mathcal{T}$
\end{document}
```

30.5   Common Symbols\Operators

```
\documentclass{article}
\begin{document}
\[\infty \]                                                           $\infty$
\[\leq, \geq, \neq, \ll, \gg \]                                       $\leq, \geq, \neq, \ll, \gg$
\[ \prec, \preceq, \succ, \succeq \]                                  $\prec, \preceq, \succ, \succeq$
\[\forall,\exists, \not\exists, \iff \]                               $\forall, \exists, \nexists, \iff$
\[\sim,\cong,\simeq,\approx,\equiv\]                                  $\sim, \cong, \simeq, \approx, \equiv$
\[\perp, \parallel,\propto, \not\perp\]                               $\perp, \parallel, \propto, \not\perp$
\[\wedge,\vee, \angle, \mid, \bigwedge, \bigvee\]                     $\wedge, \vee, \angle, \mid, \bigwedge, \bigvee$
\[\pm,\times,\ast\]                                                   $\pm, \times, *$
\[\oplus,\ominus,\otimes, \oslash, \odot\]                            $\oplus, \ominus, \otimes, \oslash, \odot$
\[\bigoplus,\bigotimes,\bigodot\]                                     $\bigoplus, \bigotimes, \bigodot$
\[\triangle,\triangleleft, \triangleright, \square\]                 $\triangle, \triangleleft, \triangleright, \square$
\[\bigtriangleup,\bigtriangledown, \circ, \bigcirc\]                 $\bigtriangleup, \bigtriangledown, \circ, \bigcirc$
\end{document}
```

30.6 Sets and Operations on Sets

```
\documentclass{article}
\begin{document}
\[\0, \in, \ni, \setminus\]          ∅, ∈, ∋, \
\[\subset, \supset, \subseteq, \supseteq\]   ⊂, ⊃, ⊆, ⊇
\[\cup, \cap, \bigcup, \bigcap\]      ∪, ∩, ⋃, ⋂
\[\sqcup, \sqcap, \bigsqcup\]         ⊔, ⊓, ⨆
\end{document}
```

30.7 Few Common Operations with AMS Package

```
\documentclass{article}
\usepackage{amsmath}
\usepackage{amssymb}
\begin{document}
\[\therefore \implies \because \]                      ∴ ⟹ ∵
\[\nless, \ngtr, \nleq, \ngeq\]                        ≮, ≯, ≰, ≱
\[\nsubseteq, \nsupseteq, \subsetneq, \supsetneq\]     ⊈, ⊉, ⊊, ⊋
\[\nmid, \nparallel, \nsim, \ncong\]                   ∤, ∦, ≁, ≇
\end{document}
```

30.8 Negating Symbols\Operators with amsmath and centernot

```
\documentclass{article}
\usepackage{amsmath}
\usepackage{amssymb}
\begin{document}
\[\centernot \implies, \centernot\iff, \centernot\mid\]      ⇏ , ⇎ , ∤
\[\centernot\perp, \centernot\equiv\]                        ⊥̸, ≢
\[\centernot\parallel, \centernot\sim, \centernot\cong\]     ∦, ≁, ≇
\end{document}
```

30.9   Bracketing

```
\documentclass{article}
\begin{document}

\[ \Biggl( \biggl( \Bigl( \bigl( ( ) \bigr) \Bigr) \biggr) \Biggr) \]

\[ \Biggl[ \biggl[ \Bigl[ \bigl[ [ ] \bigr] \Bigr] \biggr] \Biggr] \]

\[ \Biggl| \biggl| \Bigl| \bigl| | \ | \bigr| \Bigr| \biggr| \Biggr| \]

\end{document}
```

$$\left(\left(\left(\left(()\right)\right)\right)\right)$$

$$\left[\left[\left[\left[[]\right]\right]\right]\right]$$

$$\left\|\left\|\left\||\ |\right\|\right\|\right\|$$

30.10   Common Functions

```
\documentclass{article}
\begin{document}
\[\sin, \cos, \tan, \cot, \sec, \csc \]
\[\arcsin, \arccos, \arctan, \sinh, \cosh, \tanh \]
\[\log, \ln, \sup, \exp, \inf, \sup, \max, \min \]
\[a \equiv r(\bmod\; n),a \not\equiv r(\bmod\;n) \]
\end{document}
```

$$\sin, \cos, \tan, \cot, \sec, \csc$$
$$\arcsin, \arccos, \arctan, \sinh, \cosh, \tanh$$
$$\log, \ln, \sup, \exp, \inf, \sup, \max, \min$$
$$a \equiv r(\bmod\ n), a \not\equiv r(\bmod\ n)$$

30.11   Few examples of functions

```
\documentclass{article}
\usepackage{bbm}
\begin{document}
\( f: \mathbbm{R} \setminus \{0\} \to \mathbbm{R}\)
   defined as \\
\(f(x) = \frac{\sin{x}}{x} \)
\end{document}
```

$$f : \mathbb{R} \setminus \{0\} \to \mathbb{R} \text{ defined as}$$
$$f(x) = \tfrac{\sin x}{x}$$

```
\documentclass{article}
\usepackage{bbm}
\begin{document}
\( f: \mathbbm{R} \to \mathbbm{R}\) defined as \\
\(f(x) =
\left\{
 \begin{array}{ll}
 x  & \mbox{if } x \geq 0 \\
 -x & \mbox{if } x < 0
 \end{array}
\right. \)
\end{document}
```

$$f : \mathbb{R} \to \mathbb{R} \text{ defined as}$$
$$f(x) = \begin{cases} x & \text{if } x \geq 0 \\ -x & \text{if } x < 0 \end{cases}$$

30.12   Angles in Degrees

```
\documentclass{article}
\usepackage{gensymb}
\begin{document}
\[90\degree, 180\degree\]
\end{document}
```
$90°, 180°$

30.13   Absolute Values and Norms with commath package

```
\documentclass{article}
\usepackage{commath}
\begin{document}
\[\abs{x},\norm{y}, \norm{\frac{x}{\abs{y}}}\]
\end{document}
```
$|x|, \|y\|, \left\|\frac{x}{|y|}\right\|$

30.14   Accents

```
\documentclass{article}
\begin{document}
\[\bar{a},\vec{a},\hat{a}\]
```
$\bar{a}, \vec{a}, \hat{a}$

```
\[\tilde{a},\dot{a},\ddot{a}\]
```
$\tilde{a}, \dot{a}, \ddot{a}$

```
\[\check{a},\acute{a},\breve{a}\]
\end{document}
```
$\check{a}, \acute{a}, \breve{a}$

30.15   Dots, Overlines\Underlines, Overbraces\Underbraces etc.

```
\documentclass{article}
\begin{document}
\[a + b + c + \cdots \]
```
$a + b + c + \cdots$

```
\[a_0,a_1,a_2 \ldots\]
```
$a_0, a_1, a_2 \ldots$

```
\[\overline{abc}, \underline{abc}\]
```
$\overline{abc}, \underline{abc}$

```
\[\overleftarrow{abc}, \overrightarrow{abc}\]
```
$\overleftarrow{abc}, \overrightarrow{abc}$

```
\[\widetilde{abc}, \widehat{abc}\]
```
$\widetilde{abc}, \widehat{abc}$

```
\[\overbrace{abc},\underbrace{abc}\]
\end{document}
```
$\overbrace{abc}, \underbrace{abc}$

30.16   Powers, Roots and Fractions

```
\documentclass{article}
\begin{document}
\[x,y,z\]                                              x, y, z
\[x_1,y_2,z_3\]                                        x_1, y_2, z_3
\[x^2,y^2,z^2\]                                        x^2, y^2, z^2
\[x_1^2,y_2^3,z_3^4\]                                  x_1^2, y_2^3, z_3^4

\[\sqrt{x}, \sqrt[3]{x}\]                              √x, ∛x

\[\sqrt{\sqrt{\sqrt{x}}}, \sqrt[n]{x_1^2+y_2^3}\]      √√√x, ⁿ√(x_1^2+y_2^3)

\[\frac{x}{y}, \frac{\frac{a}{b}}{\frac{c}{d}}\]       x/y, (a/b)/(c/d)
\end{document}
```

x, y, z

x_1, y_2, z_3

x^2, y^2, z^2

x_1^2, y_2^3, z_3^4

$\sqrt{x}, \sqrt[3]{x}$

$\sqrt{\sqrt{\sqrt{x}}}, \sqrt[n]{x_1^2+y_2^3}$

$\frac{x}{y}, \frac{\frac{a}{b}}{\frac{c}{d}}$

30.17   Summations

```
\documentclass{article}
\begin{document}
\[\sum\]

\[\sum a + b + c + \ldots\]

\[\sum_{n=1}^{n=\infty}\frac{1}{n}\]

\[\sum\limits_{n=1}^{n=\infty}\frac{1}{n}\]

\end{document}
```

$\sum$

$\sum a + b + c + \ldots$

$\sum_{n=1}^{n=\infty} \frac{1}{n}$

$\sum\limits_{n=1}^{n=\infty} \frac{1}{n}$

Observe the use of \limits.

30.18   Binomial Coefficients

```
\documentclass{article}
\usepackage{amsmath}
\begin{document}
\[\binom{n}{r} = \frac{n!}{r!(n-r)!}\]      (n r) = n!/(r!(n-r)!)

\[^nC_r = \frac{n!}{r!(n-r)}\]              nC_r = n!/(r!(n-r))

\[^nP_r = \frac{n!}{(n-r)!} \]              ^nP_r = n!/((n-r)!)
\end{document}
```

$\binom{n}{r} = \frac{n!}{r!(n-r)!}$

$nC_r = \frac{n!}{r!(n-r)}$

$^nP_r = \frac{n!}{(n-r)!}$

30.19   Limits

```
\documentclass{article}
\begin{document}
\(\lim_{n \to \infty}\frac{1}{n} = 0\)
```
$$\lim_{n\to\infty} \frac{1}{n} = 0$$

```
\(\lim\limits_{n \to \infty}\frac{1}{n} = 0\)
```
$$\lim_{n\to\infty} \frac{1}{n} = 0$$

```
\(\lim_{n \to \infty}{(1 + \frac{1}{n})}^{n} = e\)
```
$$\lim_{n\to\infty} \left(1 + \frac{1}{n}\right)^{n} = e$$

```
\(\lim\limits_{n \to \infty}{(1 + \frac{1}{n})}^{n} = e\)
```
$$\lim_{n\to\infty} \left(1 + \frac{1}{n}\right)^{n} = e$$

```
\end{document}
```

Observe the use of \limits.

30.20   Derivatives

```
\documentclass{article}
\begin{document}
\[\frac{dy}{dx}\]
```
$$\frac{dy}{dx}$$

```
\[\frac{d^2y}{dx^2}\]
```
$$\frac{d^2y}{dx^2}$$

```
\[\frac{\partial z}{\partial x}\]
```
$$\frac{\partial z}{\partial x}$$

```
\[\frac{\partial^2 z}{\partial x^2}\]
```
$$\frac{\partial^2 z}{\partial x^2}$$

```
\[\frac{\partial^2 z}{\partial x \partial y}\]
```
$$\frac{\partial^2 z}{\partial x \partial y}$$

```
\end{document}
```

30.21   Integration

```
\documentclass{article}
\begin{document}
\[\int,\oint\]
```
$\int, \oint$

```
\[\int f(x)\,dx, \int \!f(x)\,dx\]
```
$\int f(x)\,dx, \int f(x)\,dx$

```
\[\int_{0}^{2\pi}x\,dx, \int_{0}^{2\pi}\!x\,dx \]
```
$\int_0^{2\pi} x\,dx, \int_0^{2\pi} x\,dx$

```
\[\int\limits_{0}^{2\pi}x\,dx, \int\limits_{0}^{2\pi}\!x\,dx\]
```
$\int\limits_0^{2\pi} x\,dx, \int\limits_0^{2\pi} x\,dx$

```
\[\int_{0}^{2\pi}x\,\mathrm{d}x, \int_{0}^{2\pi}\!x\,\mathrm{d}x\]
```
$\int_0^{2\pi} x\,\mathrm{d}x, \int_0^{2\pi} x\,\mathrm{d}x$

```
\[\int\limits_{0}^{2\pi}x\,\mathrm{d}x\]
```
$\int\limits_0^{2\pi} x\,\mathrm{d}x$

```
\[\int\limits_{0}^{2\pi}\!x\,\mathrm{d}x\]
```
$\int\limits_0^{2\pi} x\,\mathrm{d}x$

```
\end{document}
```

Points to Understand:

1. \! is used to reduce space between $\int$ and integrand.

2. \limits is used for proper placing of limits in inline equations.

3. \mathrm is used for proper formatting of differential d.

30.22   Double Integration

```
\documentclass{article}
\usepackage{amsmath}
\begin{document}
\[\iint, \iint f(x)\,dx\]
```
$$\iint, \iint f(x)\,dx$$

```
\[\iint f(x)\,dx\,dy\]
```
$$\iint f(x)\,dx\,dy$$

```
\[\iint_D f(x)\,dx\,dy \]
```
$$\iint_D f(x)\,dx\,dy$$

```
\[\iint\limits_D f(x)\,dx\,dy \]
```
$$\iint\limits_D f(x)\,dx\,dy$$

```
\[\int_{a}^{b}\int_{c}^{d} f(x)\,dx\,dy\]
```
$$\int_a^b \int_c^d f(x)\,dx\,dy$$

```
\[\int\limits_{a}^{b}\int\limits_{c}^{d} f(x)\,dx\,dy\]
```
$$\int\limits_a^b \int\limits_c^d f(x)\,dx\,dy$$

```
\[\iint \!f(x)\,dx\,dy\]
```
$$\iint \!f(x)\,dx\,dy$$

```
\[\iint_D \!f(x)\,dx\,dy \]
```
$$\iint_D \!f(x)\,dx\,dy$$

```
\[\iint\limits_D \!f(x)\,dx\,dy \]
```
$$\iint\limits_D \!f(x)\,dx\,dy$$

```
\[\int_{a}^{b}\int_{c}^{d}\!f(x)\,dx\,dy\]
```
$$\int_a^b \int_c^d\!f(x)\,dx\,dy$$

```
\[\int\limits_{a}^{b}\int\limits_{c}^{d} \!f(x)\,dx\,dy\]
```
$$\int\limits_a^b \int\limits_c^d \!f(x)\,dx\,dy$$

```
\[\iint_D \!f(x)\,\mathrm{d}x\,\mathrm{d}y \]
```
$$\iint_D \!f(x)\,\mathrm{d}x\,\mathrm{d}y$$

```
\[\iint\limits_D \!f(x)\,\mathrm{d}x\,\mathrm{d}y \]
```
$$\iint\limits_D \!f(x)\,\mathrm{d}x\,\mathrm{d}y$$

```
\[\int_{a}^{b}\int_{c}^{d}\!f(x)\,\mathrm{d}x\,\mathrm{d}y\]
```
$$\int_a^b \int_c^d\!f(x)\,\mathrm{d}x\,\mathrm{d}y$$

```
\[\int\limits_{a}^{b}\int\limits_{c}^{d} \!f(x)\,
\mathrm{d}x\,\mathrm{d}y\]
```
$$\int\limits_a^b \int\limits_c^d \!f(x)\,\mathrm{d}x\,\mathrm{d}y$$

```
\end{document}
```

\iint is used for triple integration.

```
\documentclass{article}
\begin{document}
\[ A = \begin{array}{cc}
a_{11} & a_{12}\\
a_{21} & a_{22}
\end{array} \]
\end{document}
```

$$A = \begin{array}{cc} a_{11} & a_{12} \\ a_{21} & a_{22} \end{array}$$

```
\documentclass{article}
\begin{document}
\[ A = \left(
\begin{array}{cc}
a_{11} & a_{12}\\
a_{21} & a_{22}
\end{array}
\right) \]
\end{document}
```

$$A = \left(\begin{array}{cc} a_{11} & a_{12} \\ a_{21} & a_{22} \end{array} \right)$$

```
\documentclass{article}
\begin{document}
\[ A = \left[
\begin{array}{cc}
a_{11} & a_{12}\\
a_{21} & a_{22}
\end{array}
\right] \]
\end{document}
```

$$A = \left[\begin{array}{cc} a_{11} & a_{12} \\ a_{21} & a_{22} \end{array} \right]$$

```
\documentclass{article}
\usepackage{amsmath}
\begin{document}
\[ A = \begin{matrix}
a_{11} & a_{12}\\
a_{21} & a_{22}
\end{matrix} \]
\end{document}
```

$$A = \begin{matrix} a_{11} & a_{12} \\ a_{21} & a_{22} \end{matrix}$$

```
\documentclass{article}
\usepackage{amsmath}
\begin{document}
\[ A = \begin{pmatrix}
a_{11} & a_{12}\\
a_{21} & a_{22}
\end{pmatrix} \]
\end{document}
```

$$A = \begin{pmatrix} a_{11} & a_{12} \\ a_{21} & a_{22} \end{pmatrix}$$

```
\documentclass{article}
\usepackage{amsmath}
\begin{document}
 \[ A = \begin{bmatrix}
a_{11} & a_{12}\\
a_{21} & a_{22}
\end{bmatrix} \]
\end{document}
```

$$A = \begin{bmatrix} a_{11} & a_{12} \\ a_{21} & a_{22} \end{bmatrix}$$

```
\documentclass{article}
\usepackage{amsmath}
\begin{document}
\[ A = \begin{vmatrix}
a_{11} & a_{12}\\
a_{21} & a_{22}
\end{vmatrix} \]
\end{document}
```

$$A = \begin{vmatrix} a_{11} & a_{12} \\ a_{21} & a_{22} \end{vmatrix}$$

```
\documentclass{article}
\usepackage{amsmath}
\begin{document}
\[ A = \begin{Vmatrix}
a_{11} & a_{12}\\
a_{21} & a_{22}
\end{Vmatrix} \]
\end{document}
```

$$A = \begin{Vmatrix} a_{11} & a_{12} \\ a_{21} & a_{22} \end{Vmatrix}$$

```
\documentclass{article}
\usepackage{amsmath}
\begin{document}
\[ A = \begin{Bmatrix}
a_{11} & a_{12}\\
a_{21} & a_{22}
\end{Bmatrix} \]
\end{document}
```

$$A = \begin{Bmatrix} a_{11} & a_{12} \\ a_{21} & a_{22} \end{Bmatrix}$$

31 User Defined Commands

```
\documentclass{article}
\begin{document}
\newcommand{\xyz}{This is user defined command.}

\xyz                                    This is user defined command.

\end{document}
```

```
\documentclass{article}
\begin{document}
\newcommand{\poly}{a_0+a_1x+\cdots+a_nx^n}

 \(\poly\)                              $a_0 + a_1x + \cdots + a_nx^n$

\end{document}
```

```
\documentclass{article}
\begin{document}
\newcommand{\polyd}[1]{a_0+a_1x+\cdots+a_#1x^#1}

\[\polyd{m}\]                           $a_0 + a_1x + \cdots + a_mx^m$

\[\polyd{n}\]                           $a_0 + a_1x + \cdots + a_nx^n$

\end{document}
```

```
\documentclass{article}
\begin{document}
\newcommand{\polyvd}[2]{a_0+a_1#1+\cdots+a_#2#1^#2}

\[\polyvd{x}{m}\]                       $a_0 + a_1x + \cdots + a_mx^m$

\[\polyvd{y}{n}\]]                      $a_0 + a_1y + \cdots + a_ny^n$

\end{document}
```

```
\documentclass{article}
\begin{document}
\newcommand{\polycvd}[3]{#1_0+#1_1#2+\cdots+#1_#3#2^#3}

\[\polycvd{a}{x}{m}\]                   $a_0 + a_1x + \cdots + a_mx^m$

\[\polycvd{b}{y}{n}\]                   $b_0 + b_1y + \cdots + b_ny^n$

\[\polycvd{c}{z}{p}\]                   $c_0 + c_1z + \cdots + c_pz^p$

\end{document}
```

Points to Understand: The command format is:

```
\newcommand{command name}[no.of arguuments]{definition}
```

1. `command name` begins with \
2. `no.of arguments` is an integer from 1 to 9.
3. #n in `definition` of command is replaced by n[th] argument.

32 Redefining Commands

```
\documentclass{article}
\begin{document}
\renewcommand{\textbf}{\textit}
\textbf{Italic text with redefined \textbackslash textbf!}
\end{document}
```
Italic text with redefined \textbf!

```
\documentclass{article}
\begin{document}
\newcommand{\xyz}{This is user defined command.}
\xyz
```
This is user defined command.
```
\renewcommand{\xyz}{This is redefined xyz command.}
\xyz
```
This is redefined xyz command.
```
\end{document}
```

```
\documentclass{article}
\begin{document}
\newcommand{\xyz}{This is user defined command.}
\xyz
```
This is user defined command.
```
\renewcommand{\xyz}[2]{A redefined xyz command of
args. #1 and #2.}
\xyz{a}{b}
```
A redefined xyz command of args. a and b
```
\end{document}
```

Points to Understand: The command format is:

`\renewcommand{command to be redefined}[no.of arguuments]{definition}`

1. `no.of arguments` is an integer from 1 to 9.
2. #n in `definition` of command is replaced by n^{th} argument.

---

33 Question Papers with Exam Document Class

```
\documentclass[addpoints,12pt]{exam}
\begin{document}
\begin{questions}
\question[10] What is the I question?
```
1. (10 points) What is the I question?
```
\question[10] What is the II question?
```
2. (15 points) What is the II question?
```
\end{questions}
\end{document}
```

```latex
\documentclass[addpoints,12pt]{exam}
\pointsinmargin
\begin{document}

\begin{questions}

\question[10] What is the I question?

\question[15] What is the II question?

\end{questions}

\end{document}
```

(10) 1. What is the I question?

(15) 2. What is the II question?

```latex
\documentclass[addpoints,12pt]{exam}
\pointsinrightmargin
\begin{document}

\begin{questions}

\question[10] What is the I question?

\question[15] What is the II question?

\end{questions}

\end{document}
```

1. What is the I question?   (10)

2. What is the II question?   (15)

```latex
\documentclass[addpoints,12pt]{exam}
\pointsinrightmargin
\begin{document}

\begin{questions}

\question[10] What is the I question?

\question
\begin{parts}

\part[5] What is I sub-question?

\part[5] What is II sub-question?

\part
\begin{subparts}

\subpart[3] What is I sub-question in (c)?

\subpart[2] What is II sub-question in (c)?

\end{subparts}

\end{parts}

\end{questions}

\end{document}
```

1. What is the I question?   (10)

2. (a) What is I sub-question?   (5)

   (b) What is II sub-question?   (5)

   (c) i. What is I sub-question in (c)?   (3)

      ii. What is II sub-question in (c)?   (2)

Points to Understand:

1. The environment \begin{questions} ... \end{questions} in *exam* document class.

2. \{pointsinrightmargin} to print marks in right margin.

3. For sub-questions:
   \begin{parts} ... \end{parts}   in   environment   \begin{questions} ... \end{questions}.

\begin{subparts} ... \end{subparts} in environment \begin{parts} ... \end{parts}.

```
\documentclass[addpoints,12pt]{exam}
\pointsinrightmargin
\begin{document}
\begin{questions}
\question[2] Which is the correct option?
\begin{choices}
\choice First Option
\choice Second Option
\choice Third Option
\choice Fourth Option
\end{choices}
\end{questions}
\end{document}
```

1. Which is the correct option?   (2)

    A. First Option
    B. Second Option
    C. Third Option
    D. Fourth Option

```
\documentclass[addpoints,12pt]{exam}
\pointsinrightmargin
\begin{document}
\begin{questions}
\question[2] Which is the correct option?\\
\begin{oneparchoices}
\choice First Option
\choice Second Option
\choice Third Option
\choice Fourth Option
\end{oneparchoices}
\end{questions}
\end{document}
```

1. Which is the correct option?   (2)

    A. First Option B. Second Option C. Third Option D. Fourth Option

```
\documentclass[addpoints,12pt]{exam}
\pointsinrightmargin
\begin{document}
\begin{questions}
\question[2] Which is the correct option?
\begin{checkboxes}
\choice First Option
\choice Second Option
\choice Third Option
\choice Fourth Option
\end{checkboxes}
\end{questions}
\end{document}
```

1. Which is the correct option?   (2)

    ○ First Option
    ○ Second Option
    ○ Third Option
    ○ Fourth Option

```
\documentclass[addpoints,12pt]{exam}
\pointsinrightmargin
\begin{document}
\begin{questions}

\question[2] Which is the correct option?\\

\begin{oneparcheckboxes}

\choice First Option
\choice Second Option

\choice Third Option

\choice Fourth Option
\end{oneparcheckboxes}
\end{questions}
\end{document}
```

1. Which is the correct option?   (2)

○ First Option ○ Second Option ○ Third
Option ○ Fourth Option

```
\documentclass[addpoints,12pt]{exam}
\usepackage{amssymb}
\checkboxchar{\(\Box \)}
\pointsinrightmargin
\begin{document}
\begin{questions}

\question[2] Which is the correct option?

\begin{checkboxes}

\choice First Option

\choice Second Option

\choice Third Option

\choice Fourth Option

\end{checkboxes}
\end{questions}
\end{document}
```

1. Which is the correct option?   (2)

□ First Option
□ Second Option
□ Third Option
□ Fourth Option

```
\documentclass[addpoints,12pt]{exam}
\usepackage{amssymb}
\checkboxchar{\(\Box \)}
\pointsinrightmargin
\begin{document}
\begin{questions}

\question[2] Which is the correct option?\\

\begin{oneparcheckboxes}

\choice First Option
\choice Second Option

\choice Third Option

\choice Fourth Option
\end{oneparcheckboxes}
\end{questions}
\end{document}
```

1. Which is the correct option?   (2)

□ First Option □ Second Option □ Third
Option □ Fourth Option

Tips:

1. \fillin for fill in the blank questions.

2. \begin{solution} ...\end{solution} to include solutions after question. The command \printanswers or \noprintanswers before question environment in order to print or no-print of solutions.

3. to include header and footer use the command \pagestyle{headandfoot} in preamble and then use \lhead{},\chead{},\rhead{},\lfoot{},\cfoot{},\rfoot{}. Also \thispagestyle{empty} to exclude header and footer on current page. You may refer to section 27.

34   Books with Book Document Class

34.1   Content Part of Book

```
\documentclass{book}
\begin{document}
\part{First Part}
\chapter{Preface}
\chapter{First main chapter}
\section{A section}
\section{Another section}
\subsection{A sub-section}
\subsubsection[Deeper level]{A
    sub-section at deeper level}
\chapter{Second main chapter}
\part{Second part}
\chapter{Third main chapter}
\chapter{Fourth main chapter}
\end{document}
```

```
\documentclass{book}
\begin{document}
\part{First Part}
\chapter*{Preface}
\chapter{First main chapter}
\section{A section}
\section{Another section}
\subsection{A sub-section}
\subsubsection[Deeper level]{A
    sub-section at deeper level}
\chapter{Second main chapter}
\part{Second part}
\chapter{Third main chapter}
\chapter{Fourth main chapter}
\end{document}
```

Tip: The package fancyhdr(section 27) may be used to set headers and footers.

34.2 Creating Title Page

```
\documentclass{book}
\begin{document}
\begin{titlepage}
\noindent{\Huge Name of Book \\ \\ }
{\large edition \\ \\ \\}
{\Large Author\\}
\vfill
{\itshape year, Publisher}
\end{titlepage}
\end{document}
```

Name of Book

edition

Author

year, Publisher

34.3 Including Table of Contents

```
\documentclass{book}
\begin{document}
\tableofcontents
\part{First Part}
\chapter*{Preface}
\chapter{First main chapter}
\section{A section}
\section{Another section}
\subsection{A sub-section}
\subsubsection[Deeper level]{A
    sub-section at deeper level}
\chapter{Second main chapter}
\part{Second part}
\chapter{Third main chapter}
\chapter{Fourth main chapter}
\section{A section in IV Chapter}
\end{document}
```

Contents

```latex
\documentclass{book}
\begin{document}
\tableofcontents
\part{First Part}
\chapter*{Preface}
\addcontentsline{toc}{chapter}{Preface}
\chapter{First main chapter}
\section{A section}
\section{Another section}
\subsection{A sub-section}
\subsubsection[Deeper level]{A
    sub-section at deeper level}
\chapter{Second main chapter}
\part{Second part}
\chapter{Third main chapter}
\chapter{Fourth main chapter}
\addtocontents{toc}{Some Description of
    Section}
\section{A section in IV Chapter}
\end{document}
```

Contents

Points to Understand:

1. \tableofcontents to inclued table of contents.

2. \addcontentsline to manually add entry in table of contents. It can be used to add entries in table of contents at any level. The command format is

   ```latex
   \addcontentsline{toc}{level}{Name of Entry}
   ```

   The level can be part, chapter, section or subsection.

3. \addcontents to manually add entry in table of contents *without* page number. The command format is

   ```latex
   \addcontents{toc}{Name of Entry}
   ```

```
\documentclass{book}
\setcounter{tocdepth}{0}
\begin{document}
\tableofcontents
\part{First Part}
\chapter*{Preface}
\addcontentsline{toc}{chapter}{Preface}
\chapter{First main chapter}
\section{A section}
\section{Another section}
\subsection{A sub-section}
\subsubsection[Deeper level]{A
    sub-section at deeper level}
\chapter{Second main chapter}
\part{Second part}
\chapter{Third main chapter}
\chapter{Fourth main chapter}
\addtocontents{toc}{Some Description}
\section{A section in IV Chapter}
\end{document}
```

Contents

```
\documentclass{book}
\setcounter{tocdepth}{1}
\begin{document}
\tableofcontents
\part{First Part}
\chapter*{Preface}
\addcontentsline{toc}{chapter}{Preface}
\chapter{First main chapter}
\section{A section}
\section{Another section}
\subsection{A sub-section}
\subsubsection[Deeper level]{A
    sub-section at deeper level}
\chapter{Second main chapter}
\part{Second part}
\chapter{Third main chapter}
\chapter{Fourth main chapter}
\addtocontents{toc}{Some Description}
\section{A section in IV Chapter}
\end{document}
```

Contents

```latex
\documentclass{book}
\usepackage{hyperref}
\setcounter{tocdepth}{1}
\begin{document}
\tableofcontents
\part{First Part}
\chapter*{Preface}
\addcontentsline{toc}{chapter}{Preface}
\chapter{First main chapter}
\section{A section}
\section{Another section}
\subsection{A sub-section}
\subsubsection[Deeper level]{A
sub-section at deeper level}
\chapter{Second main chapter}
\part{Second part}
\chapter{Third main chapter}
\chapter{Fourth main chapter}
\addtocontents{toc}{Some Description}
\section{A section in IV Chapter}
\end{document}
```

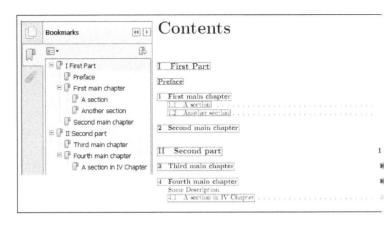

```latex
\documentclass{book}
\usepackage[colorlinks=true,
    linkcolor=blue]{hyperref}
\setcounter{tocdepth}{1}
\begin{document}
\tableofcontents
\part{First Part}
\chapter*{Preface}
\addcontentsline{toc}{chapter}{Preface}
\chapter{First main chapter}
\section{A section}
\section{Another section}
\subsection{A sub-section}
\subsubsection[Deeper level]{A
sub-section at deeper level}
\chapter{Second main chapter}
\part{Second part}
\chapter{Third main chapter}
\chapter{Fourth main chapter}
\addtocontents{toc}{Some Description}
\section{A section in IV Chapter}
\end{document}
```

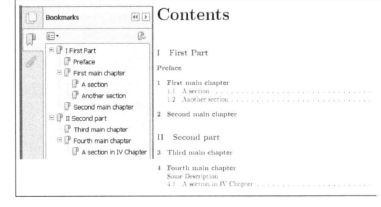

Points to Understand:

1. *hyperref* package creates auto bookmarks and hyperlinks of chapters, sections, subsections etc. It has optional arguments to change appearance of bookmarks and hyperlinks.

2. \setcounter{tocdepth}{depth level}

is used to set depth level of table of contents.

Content Part	Level
Part	-1
Chapter	0
Section	1
Subsection	2
Subsection	3
Paragraph	4
Subparagraph	5

34.4   Including List of Figures

The inclusion of list of figures(lof) is similar to inclusion of table of contents(toc).

```
\documentclass{book}
\usepackage{graphicx}
\begin{document}
\listoffigures
\part{First Part}
\chapter*{Preface}
\chapter{First main chapter}
\section{A section}
\addtocontents{lof}{some description before figure}
\begin{figure}[htbp]
\begin{center}
\fbox{\includegraphics[width=4cm, angle=0]{sample.jpg}}
\caption{Sample Figure}
\end{center}
\end{figure}
\addcontentsline{lof}{figure}{some description after figure}
\section{Another section}
\subsection{A smaller section}
\subsubsection[Deeper level]{This section has an even deeper level}
\chapter{Second main chapter}
\part{Second part}
\chapter{Third main chapter}
\end{document}
```

List of Figures

Points to Understand:

1. \listoffigures to include list of figures.

2. \addcontents to manually add entry in list of figures *without* page number. The command format is

   ```
   \addcontents{lof}{Name of Entry}
   ```

3. \addcontentsline to manually add entry in list of figures. The command format is

   ```
   \addcontentsline{lof}{figure}{Name of Entry}
   ```

34.5   Including List of Tables

The inclusion of list of tables(lot) is similar to inclusion of list of figures(lof) or table of contents(toc).

```
\documentclass{book}
\begin{document}
\listoftables
\part{First Part}
\chapter*{Preface}
\chapter{First main chapter}
\section{A section}
\addtocontents{lot}{some description before table}
\begin{table}[htbp]
\begin{tabular}{ccc}
\hline
\textbf{Col. 1} & \textbf{Col. 2} & \textbf{Col. 3} \\
\hline
11 & 12 & 13 \\
\hline
21 & 22 & 23 \\
\hline
31 & 32 & 33 \\
\hline
```

```
\end{tabular}
\centering
\caption{Table Name}
\end{table}
\addcontentsline{lot}{table}{some desription after table}
\section{Another section}
\subsection{A smaller section}
\subsubsection[Deeper level]{This section has an even deeper level}
\chapter{Second main chapter}
\part{Second part}
\chapter{Third main chapter}
\end{document}
```

List of Tables

some description before table

Points to Understand:

1. `\listoftables` to include list of tables.

2. `\addcontentsline` to manually add entry in list of tables. The command format is

   ```
   \addcontentsline{lot}{table}{Name of Entry}
   ```

3. `\addcontents` to manually add entry in list of tables *without* page number. The command format is

   ```
   \addcontents{lot}{Name of Entry}
   ```

34.6 Index with Index Package

```
\documentclass{book}
\usepackage{index}
\makeindex
\begin{document}
\part{First Part}
\chapter*{Preface}
\chapter{First main chapter}
\section{A section}
\index{index entry A}
\section{Another section}
\subsection{A smaller section}
\chapter{Second main chapter}
\part{Second part}
\index{index entry B}
\chapter{Third main chapter}
\index{index entry C}
\index{index entry A}
\printindex
\end{document}
```

```
\documentclass{book}
\usepackage{index}
\makeindex
\begin{document}
\part{First Part}
\chapter*{Preface}
\chapter{First main chapter}
\section{A section}
\index{index entry A}
\section{Another section}
\subsection{A smaller section}
\chapter{Second main chapter}
\part{Second part}
\index{index entry B}
\chapter{Third main chapter}
\index{index entry C}
\index{index entry A}
\index{index entry D |see{index entry C}}
\printindex
\end{document}
```

Index

index entry A, 5, 11

index entry B, 11

index entry C, 11

Index

index entry A, 5, 11

index entry B, 11

index entry C, 11

index entry D , *see* index entry C

Points to Understand:

1. \printindex with *index* package to include index.

2. Include \makeindex in preamble of document.

3. \index to add entry in list of index. The command format is

   \index{Index Entry} OR \index{Index Entry|see{other Index Entry}}

```
\documentclass{book}                          \documentclass{book}
\usepackage{graphicx,index}                   \usepackage{index}
\makeindex                                     \makeindex
\begin{document}                               \begin{document}
\part{First Part}                              \part{First Part}
\chapter*{Preface}                             \chapter*{Preface}
\chapter{First main chapter}                   \chapter{First main chapter}
\section{A section}                            \section{A section}
\index{index entry A}                          \index{index entry A}
\section{Another section}                       \section{Another section}
\subsection{A smaller section}                 \subsection{A smaller section}
\chapter{Second main chapter}                  \chapter{Second main chapter}
\part{Second part}                             \part{Second part}
\index{index entry B}                          \index{index entry B}
\begin{figure}[htbp]                           \begin{table}[htbp]
\begin{center}                                 \begin{tabular}{ccc}
\fbox{\includegraphics[width=4cm,             \hline
    angle=0]{sample.jpg}}                       11 & 12 & 13 \\
\caption{\index{some figure}Sample Figure}     \hline
\end{center}                                    21 & 22 & 23 \\
\end{figure}                                    \hline
\chapter{Third main chapter}                   \end{tabular}
\index{index entry C}                          \centering
\index{index entry A}                          \caption{\index{some table}Sample Table}
\index{index entry D |see{index entry C}}      \end{table}
\printindex                                     \chapter{Third main chapter}
\end{document}                                  \index{index entry C}
                                                \index{index entry A}
                                                \index{index entry D |see{index entry C}}
                                                \printindex
                                                \end{document}
```

Index

index entry A, 5, 13
index entry B, 11
index entry C, 13
index entry D , *see* index entry C

some figure, 11

Index

index entry A, 5, 13
index entry B, 11
index entry C, 13
index entry D , *see* index entry C

some table, 11

Point to Understand:

```
\caption{\index{Index Entry}Figure Name\Table Name}
```

to include figure or table in index.

34.7 Including Bibliography

```
\documentclass{book}
\begin{document}
\part{First Part}
\chapter*{Preface}
\chapter{First main chapter}
\section{A section}
\section{Another section}
\subsection{A smaller section}
You may refer to \cite{Ref1} and also to \cite{Ref2}.
\chapter{Second main chapter}
\part{Second part}
\chapter{Third main chapter}
\begin{thebibliography}{99}
\bibitem{Ref1} Author 1., \textit{Book 1}, Publisher 1, Year 1.
\bibitem{Ref2} Author 2., \textit{Book 2}, Publisher 2, Year 2.
\end{thebibliography}
\end{document}
```

Bibliography

[1] Author 1., *Book 1*, Publisher 1, Year 1.

[2] Author 2., *Book 2*, Publisher 2, Year 2.

```
\documentclass{book}
\begin{document}
\part{First Part}
\chapter*{Preface}
\chapter{First main chapter}
\section{A section}
\section{Another section}
You may refer to \cite{Ref1} and also to \cite{Ref2}.
\chapter{Second main chapter}
\part{Second part}
\chapter{Third main chapter}
\begin{thebibliography}{99}
\bibitem[Label 1]{Ref1} Author 1., \textit{Book 1}, Publisher 1, Year 1.
\bibitem[Label 2]{Ref2} Author 2., \textit{Book 2}, Publisher 2, Year 2.
\end{thebibliography}
\end{document}
```

Bibliography

[Label 1] Author 1., *Book 1*, Publisher 1, Year 1.

[Label 2] Author 2., *Book 2*, Publisher 2, Year 2.

Points to Understand:

1. The environment `\begin{thebibliography}` ... `\end{thebibliography}` to include *thebibliography*. The command format is

   `\begin{thebibliography}{widest-label}`

   widest-label is as wide as the widest item label produces by the \bibitem. It can be number or text.

2. The command format to include bibliographic items is

   `\bibitem[label]{cite_key}`

34.8   Including Appendices

```
\documentclass{book}
\begin{document}
\tableofcontents
\part{First Part}
\chapter*{Preface}
\addcontentsline{toc}{chapter}{Preface}
\chapter{First main chapter}
\section{A section}
\section{Another section}
\subsection{A smaller section}
\chapter{Second main chapter}
\part{Second part}
\chapter{Third main chapter}
\appendix
\cleardoublepage
\addtocontents{toc}{\bigskip}
\addcontentsline{toc}{part}{Appendix}
\chapter{Glossary}
\chapter{Symbols}
\end{document}
```

Contents

> **Points to Understand:**
>
> 1. A chapter after command `\appendix` is included as appendix.
>
> 2. `\cleardoublepage` clears the current page and makes the next non-float page at right hand in two-sided layout. Also `\clearpage` ends the current page.
>
> 3. `\bigskip` to add vertical space in table of contents.

35 A simple Research Article

The most of the thing that are described in *section 30: Books with book document class* apply to *article* class too. For example, creating *table of contents, list of figures, list of tables, bibliography etc.* Here is a simple template of research article.

```
\documentclass[letterpaper]{article}
\usepackage{geometry,url,graphicx}
\title{A Sample Research Paper}
\author{X Y Z}
\date{dd-mm-yyyy}
\begin{document}
\maketitle
\abstract{An abstract}
\newpage
\tableofcontents
\newpage
\listoffigures
\newpage
\listoftables
\newpage
\section{Introduction}
 An Introduction.
\section{Background and Preliminary}
A Background and Prelimnary
\section{First Main Section}
A first section
\subsection{Subsection of I Section}
A subsection
\subsection{Another Subsection of I Section}
Another subsection
\section{Second Main Section}
A second section
\subsection{Subsection of II Section}
A subsection
\subsection{Another Subsection of II Section}
Another subsection
\section{Conclusion}
A conclusion
\newpage
\begin{thebibliography}{99}
```

```
\bibitem{Ref1} Author 1., \textit{Book 1}, Publisher 1, Year 1.
\bibitem{Ref2} Author 2., \textit{Book 2}, Publisher 2, Year 2.
\end{thebibliography}
\end{document}
```

A Sample Research Paper

X Y Z

dd-mm-yyyy

Abstract

An abstract

Tip: The package `fancyhdr`(section 27) may be used to set headers and footers.

36   A simple Letter

```
\documentclass{letter}
\signature{Your name}
\address{From: \\Line 1 \\ Line 2 \\
    Line 3}
\begin{document}
\begin{letter}{To:\\ Line 1 \\ Line 2
    \\ Line 3}
\opening{Dear Sir\textbackslash Madam,}
A content part
\closing{Yours Faithfully,}
\ps{P.S. Here goes your ps.}
\encl{Enclosures.}
\end{letter}
\end{document}
```

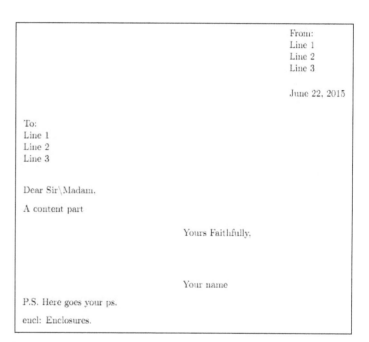

Tip: Use package `fancyhdr` to set header and footer. You may have to use `\thispagestyle{fancy}` to include header and footer on current page. You may refer to section 27.

37   Including Other Documents\Files

While creating large documents, it becomes easier to divide document in parts and then include these parts in root file. The following commands can be used to do this.

1. `\input{filename}`. For example you may type preamble in separate file say named "01.tex" and then include it in your root file as `\input{01}`. The file 01 is assumed to be in the same folder where root `tex` file is. A simple splitting of document in this way may loose cross-referencing.

2. `\include{filename}`. It works like `\input{filename}` but for the fact that it begins inclusion on next page and also forces next part of document to begin on fresh page. Further it can't be used in preamble of document.

38 Concluding Remarks

LaTeX is very rich in its arguments. It is highly customisable. Given a task, it can be achieved in n number of ways. This guide was just meant to introduce some of the common ways of doing common tasks in LaTeX. A book recommended for further reading is "LaTeX: Beginners Guide" by *Stefan Kottwitz*.

A website `tex.stackexchange.com` would be quite helpful for mastering LaTeX.

www.ingramcontent.com/pod-product-compliance
Lightning Source LLC
Chambersburg PA
CBHW060501060326
40689CB00020B/4602